SPAIN

BERT SCHIERBEEK

photographs by
KEES SCHERER

 FOLLETT PUBLISHING COMPANY
Chicago - New York

The publishers gratefully acknowledge the help of the Spanish National Tourist Office in the preparation of the English edition.

First published in Great Britain in 1967
© 1967 C.I.B. The Hague, Holland
English translation by Joe Foster
© 1967 Methuen & Co. Ltd.
Printed in Holland
Library of Congress Catalog Card number 66 23813
Follett Publishing Company
1010 West Washington Boulevard
Chicago, Illinois 60607
8222

Lay-out: D. Ludwig

CONTENTS

Spain stretches from the Pyrenees in the north to the straits of Gibraltar in the south. It is bounded on the east by the Mediterranean Sea, on the west by the Atlantic Ocean and Portugal, and to the north by the Bay of Biscay and France. It is a large country full of alternations and contrasts in landscape, climate and population.

In the north-west the climate is a maritime one, and it rains a good deal; the central part of the country has a continental climate, with hot summers and cold winters; and on the Mediterranean coast the climate is sub-tropical. In Spain, one can ski in the Pyrenees, on the Picos de Europa (the highest parts of the Cantabrian Mountains in the north-west), in the Guadarrama mountains (right in the centre of Spain) and on the Sierra Nevada near Granada in the south. One can bathe in the Mediterranean until far into the winter and suffer from the cold in Madrid, which lies in the middle of the Meseta, the huge plateau that seems to survey the whole of Spain. One can fish for trout in the numerous streams which flow down from the mountains into the big rivers and thirst for a drop of water in Estremadura. There the land can be dry, yellow, red and grey from the dust and as endless as a desert; then suddenly the plateau is cut through by a deep-lying river, and oases of fertility appear.

The big rivers are the Ebro, which flows into the Mediterranean near Tortosa; the Douro (or Duero), which rises to the north-west of Soria in the mountains of Old Castile and flows westward past Valladolid and through Portugal to Oporto on the Atlantic; the Tagus (or Tajo), which has its source halfway between Madrid and the Mediterranean and flows past Toledo right across Spain to Lisbon; and the Guadalquivir, which runs from the La Sagra mountains through Córdoba and Seville to the Gulf of Cádiz. Yet in spite of these rivers Spain is a dry land. Deforestation caused erosion, wind and rain washed the mountains bare, and sheep and goats did the rest. It is thus not surprising that the Ministry of Agriculture in Madrid publicizes every-

5

where 'the battie against erosion' and promotes new planting.

The history of Spain is no less varied than the Spanish landscape. Because of the country's favourable position and its minerals it was coveted by many different people and partly or wholly occupied by them for longer or shorter periods. It was for Spain that the Punic Wars were waged, and Carthaginians, Greeks and Romans all established themselves in the country, the Romans for several hundred years. Celts and Normans pushed their way into the north. All these peoples left their marks on the country, its population, its economy and its culture. But it was the Moors who stayed longest in Spain. From 711, when they landed in southern Spain, to the fall of Granada in 1492, large areas of the country were ruled by the Moors. They strongly influenced Spanish life and left a stamp on Spanish culture; even today one sometimes has the impression of being in a 'non European' country.

Entering Spain from the north one is overcome by a feeling not produced by crossing the Alps into Italy. Italy is an annexe of Europe; Spain is an annexe of Africa. The *Reconquista*, the reconquest of Spain from the Moors, began from the north; it was a bloody struggle that lasted for centuries and finally ended, under the Catholic monarchs, Ferdinant of Aragon and Isabella of Castile, in the fall of Granada and the definitive formation of the Spanish state. The nature of this struggle was such that many parts of Spain always retained a certain independence vis-à-vis the central government. For the Spainiards are federalists rather than nationalists, socialists or anarchists rather than communists. The drop of Moorish blood which they almost all have makes most of them extremists. For the expulsion of the Moors did not mean the end of Moorish influence. The Moors had come as soldiers, without their womenfolk; most of them were Berbers from North Africa. They married Spanish women, and as a result their grip on Spanish life continued from one generation to the next. It is probably thanks to this that Moors and Christians often lived and worked together in an enviable spirit of tolerance. The Moors had arrived at the zenith of their civilization and could afford to be tolerant. It was they who brought the classical literatures of Greece and Rome from the libraries of Cairo. They tolerated the great Jewish scholars. They encouraged all forms of learning and research. They brought the Renaissance to Spain some centuries before its official beginning in Italy and the rest of Europe. Moors and Gypsies strongly influenced Spanish music and dancing. One can still hear the effects of this fortunate influence today, although it is apparent from the performances of the *Coros y Danzas de España* how different and how individual the music from all parts of Spain is. Amid all the strife, turbulence and conquests the isolation of the various different parts of the country always remained the most constant element. Its individual character was thus long preserved, in spite of all the international influences to which it was exposed. Among these were also the crusades and pilgrimages, especially the pilgrimage to Santiago de Compostela, to Saint James. 'Santiago' was the war-cry that heralded the *Reconquista* everywhere. It was the war-cry of the Catholicism that drove the Moors out of the country. This cry also marked the start of the Inquisition, the establishment of a central authority that tried to lop off local freedoms and to secure as swiftly as possible a liquidation of Moorish, Jewish and other minorities often the most progressive groups. The country was divided up among the noblemen who had taken part in the struggle, and the basis was thus laid of that large-scale ownership of land which still stands in the way even now of the modernization of agriculture.

Granada fell in 1492. In the same year Columbus discovered America and soon afterwards the conquest of Central and South America began. It was a campaign marked by the search for adventure and gold, but also by a holy ardour to convert the conquered territories to Christianity. Of the gold, little is left. In the wars which Spain waged to satisfy the private whims of her kings, and not least to stem the advance of Protestantism, the gold soon disappeared, but thanks to Spanish religious zeal the peoples of Central and South America, at any rate in the long run, learned the Spanish language. As a result, Spanish became one of the great languages of the world and of trade.

Universities were swiftly founded, and priests tried to save something of the old civilizations which were trampled underfoot by the *conquistadores*.

Ferdinand was succeeded in 1516 by Charles V, a Hapsburg — the son of Philip the Fair and Joanna the Mad — who in 1519 became emperor of Germany. Once again, as so often in her history, Spain was governed on principles which had nothing to do with the interests of the Spanish people but which suited the imperialist aims of Charles V. The long war which his son, Philip II, waged against the Dutch formed a part of this imperialism which the anti-Protestant struggle dictated by religious zeal made so expensive; as a result supremacy in the Mediterranean area was allowed to trickle away, and the wars in Europe were lost into the bargain.

After that Spain sank back into the ranks of the third-class nations. She had been exhausted by wars, corruption and bad government. Since then, in the eyes of the Spaniard 'the devil lives in Madrid', and he tries by every possible means to elude the net that is spun there. The enthusiastic start seldom leads to the completed task. The process is interrupted by violence. The last time that this happened was in the Civil War of 1936 to 1939. Franco won this bloody struggle with the help of Italians and Germans. The Republicans' ambitious plan to turn impoverished Spain into a modern democracy in as short a time as possible miscarried. The élan was crushed. However, the Spaniards themselves do not collapse so quickly. Organization is simply not their strong point. They are less interested in affairs of state than in life itself. We said that Spain is different, and it is different above all because of its inhabitants. We shall see this as soon as we enter the country.

1. A detail from one of the richly ornamented main doors of Tarragona Cathedral

2. View across the bay of Tossa de Mar on the Costa Brava

3. The beach at Tossa de Mar

4. Meeting under one of the characteristic little gates in the fishing village of Cadaqués, on the Costa Brava

5. Towards sunset the fishermen put out to sea to fish with the aid of searchlights

6.   The little harbour of Cadaqués

7. Fishermen on the beach near Blanes
8. Alicante
9. In the 'Barrio Gotico' (the Gothic quarter) of Barcelona
    stands the 13th-century cathedral, with its 20th-century spire

10.   Sitges, a picturesque village to the south of Barcelona

11.   The beach at Sitges

13. 13th-century statues in the doorway
◀ 12. Façade and doorway of Tarragona cathedral

14.   The 'Penon' or Great Rock of Ifach

15.   The octagonal tower ('Miguele') of Valencia Cathedral
16.   Oranges from the groves round Valencia   ▶

THE COSTA BRAVA AND THE MEDITERRANEAN COAST

A book written by a Frenchman in 1932 deals with the whole of Spain except the Costa Brava. The author did not go there and apparently no one else did either. The mass tourism did not exist, though the Costa Brava's position today is mainly due to the tourist. In those days people did not go with their whole families to lie on the seashore; that was the prerogative of individuals with enough money for it, and they went mainly in the winter to enjoy the mild climate, not to get a suntan.

But now when you enter Spain — or rather Catalonia, for the Catalans are the Welsh, so to speak, of Spain — via Port Bou, resort follows resort, all of them situated on little bays carved out of the blue sea by the foothills of the Pyrenees. A narrow, winding road leads you along the coast. Sun and natural beauty look the same as they do in France, but the people no longer speak French; they speak Catalán, which is a language — not a dialect — even though the Catalans can all speak Spanish as well. The customs officials who let you through up in the mountains by Port Bou speak Spanish in any case.

The Costa Brava (Wild Coast) is fully entitled to its name. Often the rough mountain ridges drop steeply into the sea, and in January and February storms can lash the sea into a fury; then the fishermen shelter in their villages, which in summer are full of visitors. In winter the hotels and boarding houses stand empty. Perhaps it would be an idea to go there then. Spaniards always make you heartily welcome. They are fond of people. Naturally they also want to earn something, but they are not swindlers by nature and they are more interested in people than in money. When you arrive in a place like Cadaqués, beautifully situated, you may well be involved, if you speak a little Spanish, in a conversation that usually begins like this: 'Have you ever been in Spain before? No? Or in Cadaqués? No? Oh, then you must see our church, this house, that square, the bull-ring' — in a word, everything. And you may come across the *sardana* being danced in the village square. This is an exceptionally rhythmic and lively round dance in which the whole village takes part. You can tell from the preparations that the dance is going to take place. Towards twelve o'clock the square is still empty. Suddenly along comes a group of people with musical instruments. They build a simple stand of planks and take their seats on it. Then they just wait; but swiftly men and woman, boys and girls come out of all the cafés, out of the offices and busineses. They fill the square, chattering nineteen to the dozen. The words shoot past your ears like machine-gun bullets. Spaniards like talking, and they talk loudly and at each other. But then the music begins and suddenly the conversations stop; people arrange themselves in a circle and begin to dance, to the music of blaring trumpets, drums and trombones. You are the witness of an inspired communual dance, a dance in which the cares of the day are forgotten and in which people forget themselves too, carried away in a great rhythmic ensemble which lifts them above themselves. If you are lucky you will meet it in many squares, and in any case on a Sunday in the Plaza de Cataluña in Barcelona.

From Cadaqués, one of many places that we could name, the road leads south through Rosas. But perhaps it is worth-while leaving the coast, especially since to the south south from Figueras to Gerona, another beautiful town with a splendid stately square, old at the centre and bustling of Rosas it becomes a bit swampy, and driving to Figueras, a beautiful old little town, with a splendid, cosy square, where there is peace and quiet and good food too. Then with industry on the outskirts. From Gerona one can then drive due south so as to reach Barcelona as quickly as possible; but one can also take a more northerly route that leads, northward again, to the coast, to Palamós, and then drops down, past resorts like San Feliú, Tossa de Mar, Blanes and San Pol de Mar, to Barcelona, the capital of Catalonia.

After Madrid Barcelona is the biggest city in Spain, with a population of about a million and a half. It is the centre of the textile industry, of heavy industry and of commerce. For the tourist, the old centre of the city is full of life and of things worth seeing. For one can meet — once, at any rate — a large proportion of the population of Barcelona on the Rambla de las Flores, a busy boulevard full of people and flower-stalls. Rightly called a boulevard of flowers, it divides the old city into two parts. It runs from the Plaza de Cataluña, a huge square and centre of activitiy, down to the harbour. On each side there are shops and cafés, cinemas and banks. Here — more in the cafés than in the banks — affairs are discussed and decided. For the Spaniard is fond of café life, and in this point the Catalán is no different from other Spaniards. And one must also turn off left and right from the Rambla into the little streets of the *bassio gótico* the old Gothic quarter with its splendid cathedral.

Here one can see for the first time the pomp and splendour, the gaiety and excess of Spanish altars. The are other churches too: Santa Maria del Mar, which dates from the fourteenth century, and S. Pablo del Campo, a twelfth-century building. Naturally there are the museums, a museum of modern art and one of the arts of Catalonia, and there is also the city hall, the Ayuntamiento. But above all one must not forget, after the sight-seeing, to turn off into the old quarters with their hundreds of cafés. They all start to fill up towards seven o'clock in the evening. It is then that Spaniards take their apéritif, with a *tapa*, a snack a piece of sausage, an olive, a tiny fried fish, brown beans in a piquant sauce, fried mussels, bits of fried liver, little meat balls, shrimps and many other things. All in small quantities, at prices from two to ten pesetas. You can drink cognac, wine - white, red or rosé, all varieties of sherry and indeed any drink from any part of the world at a bargain price. And if you go regularly into the same bar the barman, too, or the proprietor will take you into his confidence — something which he did not do the first time. He will offer you a drink and make you feel that you are no longer just a customer, but also a guest. For although the Catalans are typical federalsts, good business men with an outstanding feeling for profitable deals, strongly convinced of the beauty of their city and of its importance to Spain, with eyes wide open to the modern world, they are also very much tied to old traditions, and one of these is that one must behave courteously to a stranger. They live in a busy, over-populated, lively city. They have their work to do and like everyone else they think mainly of themselves. But Barcelona's long history as a cultured commercial city cannot be disowned, and this glorious history has its effect on the everyday dealings of each one of its citizens.

One must naturally also visit the Tibidabo, so as to be able to look down from above on this huge city — a working city, a cultured city, a city with its own place in the turbulent history of Spain, a city much fought over because of its position, and above all a progressive city, which has always given, and indeed still gives, its rulers, including Franco, the most trouble. Harbours, docks, factories and cathedrals ... and also that miraculous work of the sur-realist architect, Gaudi, the cathedral of the *Sagrada Familia*,

the Holy Family. This architect also built houses on the Paseo de Gracia, in the Guell Park and in la Pedrera; they are all of a bizarre baroque form, strange pieces of sculpture rather than architecture, but impressive in their imaginative conception and technical virtuosity — Art Nouveau with a decidedly Spanish slant. Gaudi used to walk along the streets reading; every tram-drver knew this, but one day a new driver was not prepared for it, ran Gaudi over, and Gaudi was no more.

You must also visit the Montjuich, another of Barcelona's hills; you go up it by rack-railway and enjoy a beautiful view straight over the sea — with a dry sherry into the bargain. Glorious!

From Barcelona a journey of forty miles in a westerly direction brings you to Montserrat, a range of mountains that thrust their inhospitable peaks more than three thousand feet into the heavens. There in the mountains lies the monastery of Montserrat, with its *Virgen Morena* (Black Virgin). Here according to folklore the Holy Grail is preserved, and so is one of the best traditions of Christianity, namely the preaching of toleration towards those of other beliefs, a tradition which right up until today has put the monastery in ill odour with the rulers of the country.

In the monastery there is a restaurant, a bar and a grocer's shop. There are a few hotels round about. And the Black Virgin, popularly known as la Morena, sits alone there on her throne amid the barren rocks and grieves for the times of the holy hermits who, far above the beaten tracks of the world and therefore secure from it, led their solitary lives and worked for a different kingdom.

We go on now southward from Barcelona. We pass first through the Piñedas, the pine woods that stretch from a sort of dune landscape down to the sea. It is an ideal holiday area, full of camping sites and hotels, both epuipped with all possible comforts. Via Castelldefels and a high, twisting coastal road we arrive in Sitges, ten years ago not much more than a fishing village, with a charming little white church by the sea, but now an important resort, visited by a great many people in the season.

After Sitges we pass through many *playas* (beaches, or resorts), such as those of Segur and Camaruga, and also through the Arco Romano de Bara, a Roman triumphal arch. After Torredembara we come to another tower, the Torre de los Escipiones, the tower of the Scipios, father and son, two Roman generals who fought here against the advancing Carthaginians in the time of the Punic Wars. Then we approach Tarragona, with its Balcon del Mediterraneo, the end of the Boulevard Generalisimo Franco. It is indeed a balcony, starting hundreds of feet above the sea dropping steeply down to the shore. This *Rambla* — a splendid name, in which one can hear the tramping of feet and the 'r's' rolling out of the mouths of busily gesticulating Spaniards — is a wide boulevard where, as in Barcelona, a great deal of the city's life is carried on. It is always overflowing with life. On both sides of it there are cafés with great rows of tables outside, not to mention the always impressive, if to our way of thinking over-size, bank buildings. But the Spaniards are fond of size. We camped for a time in the neighbourhood of Tarragona and came in every day to the Rambla about six o'clock to have an electric shave in our favourite café. That led to many conversations and to friendship with the proprieter. No Spaniard found it strange that one was busy with one's toilet in the midst of them. Nothing human is strange to them. Perhaps history has something to do with this. Take the history of Tarragona, for example: the city was often laid waste, by the Visigoths, by the Moors, even by the English in 1705, and by the French in 1811. It also suffered comparatively recently in the civil war. A. history like this puts its stamp on peoples lives and their attitude to life. They become accustomed to the vicissitudes of fate and are not so quickly astonished, even though on the other hand they get excited and continually talk about things both great and small in bombastic fashion. But this is only on the surface. They are fond of the extreme because it is one of the embellishments of life, and they are fond of embellishment because

Seville ▶

life without it is worthless. For there is a strange melancholy about his lot in the Spaniard, though he will not surrender to it. He would rather stamp the ground in fierce dances and defy life with head held high than admit the 'essential impossibility of this existence'. Only poets do this in their weak moments, and that is why Spaniards are fond of their poets and why they are able to quote from them; that is why in times of real fury they can attack a tank with a pitch-fork, and why they are as fond of Don Quixote as of Sancho Panza: they know that they both sprang from the same person, and that they themselves could have been that person.

Tarragona is a city of about 50.000 inhabitants. Once it was a flourishing Roman port. The two Scipios captured the town from the Iberians, the original inhabitants, in 218 B.C. The emperor Augustus spent a winter there. In those days the town was known as Tarraco. Many well-to-do Romans later followed their emperor's example. First one should take a trip through the old city, with its steep little streets and many cafés full of the most splendid *tapas*. Do it in the evening, and you will get the feel of the city's turbulent history, that still broods in dark little shops, in long, narrow rooms that look not so much likes cafés as cellars for wines, barrels of which stand piled along the wales. On

each side there are wooden seats, all occupied by Spaniards drinking their wine good-naturedly from funnels. They hold their fingers under the opening, let the funnel fill up, raise the spout above their mouths and let the wine run in. From outside it looks a dingy throng, but in fact it is a sociable, hearty, happy and courteous society full of mutual pleasure and always ready to offer you a drink. This lasts for an hour or two after work and then they go home to eat. The wine does not cost much; it cannot, for people do not earn very much. Although in recent years wages have certainly risen they are still far below the level of those in most other European countries. Spaniards know this perfectly well. For centuries they have purchased their personal freedom with varying degrees of hunger. They have also always staked their personal freedom to gain more elbow-room within the possible and impossible governments that they have had. Blood and tears moulded the history of Spain, and they were the result of furious personal courage and love of freedom. These people cannot be brought to heel by any government, and these are the people who welcome you and who will steal your heart for ever.

In these old quarters, the heart of Tarragona, History lives on. You can see it in the splendid façade of the cathedral that stands out above the city, a rose-coloured façade erected on the spot where once a temple of Jupiter stood. Broad steps lead up to the square in front of it, that form the foundation of many small, narrow, friendly streets leading off in all directions. Go there, and sit and look and listen; but we must continue on our way. To the south of Tarragona, on a sandy cape with beautiful beaches, lies the seaside resort of Salou, and a little further south Cambrils. And after that the road goes past more and more camping sites and beaches via Hospitalet, Vinaroz and Benicásim to Castellón de le Plana. Castellón de la Plana itself, a town of 60,000 inhabitants, is a real garden city, situated amid hundreds of *huertas* (market-gardens, orange groves, lemon groves and vineyards) with a glorious mild climate.

After only a short stop here we go on past the old Roman
city of Saguntum, now Sagunto. The ruins of the old Roman
fortifications lie up on the hill. The old city was captured
from the Romans by Hannibal in 219 B.C. The inhabitants
destroyed their goods and chattels and committed mass
suicide. Such was the Spain of days gone by, but this
pride is not alien to the Spaniard of to-day.

Now on to Valencia, with more and more rice fields on
the sea side, more and more orange and lemon groves
on the land side. We arrive in the third city of Spain, a
city of 500.000 inhabitants. Valencia is a beautiful and
distinguished city with a splendid old centre. It is ochre
in colour and its bustling inhabitants are dark-complexioned.

The Rio Turia flows round it. Drive in past the Torres de Servanor, an old gateway in the fortifications, and on into the centre, the Plaza del Caudillo. In the time of the civil war this was the last bulwark of the lawful republican government. The city suffered a good deal of damage in those days — you can still see bullet-holes in the building. But life went on; the *paella* remained the same. Paella is the great rice dish of Valencia indeed of Spain as a whole. All the fish (mussels, lobsters, octopuses etc.) in the sea, or at any rate all the meat to be found on them, go into it. It makes a rich meal. Only when you have eaten it do you fully understand the need for the siesta. There is an atmosphere of sub-tropical luxuriance, mingled nevertheless with the feeling of a great and prosperous past, to which the cathedral with its octagonal tower of Miguelete, named after St. Michael, and the Lonja de Seda, the silk exchange, a huge Gothic hall on two rows of strong but elegant pillars, transparent and light, bear witness. The silk industry is no longer so important, but fruit and rice are. They are exported through the harbour of Grao de Valencia, which lies a few miles from the city. The city's most famous fiestas are the *fallas,* a big fancy-dress procession on the 19th March, and the Battle of Flowers in July. In the Museum of Fine Arts you can see works of the medieval primitives, of the Valencia school, of Ribera, El Greco, Van Dyck and various modern painters. There is also an important ceramics industry in Valencia; some of its finest products are to be seen in the Museo Nacional de Cerámica. Besides tiles, which one no longer encounters in their old shapes and designs, the industry produced, and still produces, the stone pots and pans (*ollas*) which are used everywhere on wood fires.

There are two roads from Valencia to Alicante, one through the interior, via Alcoy, a splendid route that provides a change from coastal scenery. It enables you at any rate to learn something of the 'real' Spain, not just the face that Spain turns to its tourists. But the journey along the Costa Blanca is certainly beautiful. On the promontory of

Calpe rises the rock of Ifach, a burnt-out volcano nearly a thousand feet high, at the foot of which the Ministry of Tourism has built an *Albergue* (inn). It is plesant to rest there on the broad terraces. After Calpe one passes through Altea, where many artists work for a few months in the year. Once past Benidorm we follow the coastal road, to arrive via San Juan in Alicante.

Alicante is the city of palm trees. Nowhere can one see so many palms as in this city. All the boulevards are planted with them, They give the city an exceptionally southern look. Sit down on the splendid Esplanade, drink a cup of coffee and have your shoes cleaned; they must be pretty dirty by now. Take a walk under the palms on the beautiful mosaic pavement. Visit the market too; it is full of life. You can buy anything from food to shoes and ornaments. After·that, you can have another good rest on the Avenida Nuñes Mendez and watch the southern bustle — and idle lounging. In the evening, go into the old town or to Castillo Santa Barbara, whence there is a splendid view over the city and its natural harbour.

17.   A secluded bay near Nerja on the Costa del Sol

19.   One of the modern hotels on the Costa del Sol, near Marbella
18.   Salobreña, Costa del Sol

20. A typical balcony in the south
21. The deep gorge that divides the town of Ronda into two parts

22.   The road leading to the blue mountains of the Sierra Nevada

23. Under the sun of Ronda man and horse cast scarcely any shadow

24.   Purullena, close to Cadiz, lies in a great canyon-like landscape

25. People dig out their houses from the red volcanic rock

26. A superb piece of Moorish architecture in the Alhambra at Granada

27. The patio with the lions in the Alhambra
28. Cypresses and roses in the Generallife, the summer residence of the old kings of Granada ▶
29. 'Who can imagine the fragrance of an open rose? ▶

30.   Gypsy girl dancing and singing by the caves of the Sacro
      Monte in Granada

31.　'Dance, gypsy, dance... until the wind whirls you away'

32.   Bullfight in the arena at Granada

We go on now to Andalusia and the Costa del Sol. In Murcia we just spare the time to look at the cathedral, which was begun in 1394 on the spot where a mosque once stood. Under the Moors, Murcia was known as Mursiya. Moorish influence can be seen everywhere, in the gables of the houses that line the narrow, winding little streets. It is also visible in the glittering black eyes of the people of Murcia, in their rapid, fluid gestures, their language and their habits of life. Here the siesta is more sacred than in the north. Here work is more of a burden than a joy. Here the sun blazes down on the human skin and on the earth. But the surrounding area is one big garden, thanks to the waters of the Rio Sagura. If you follow the river inland a little way, you will see orange trees and date palms growing between the steep, bare mountains, splendid gardens with all kinds of southern fruits — in short a brilliant use of water.

The road to the south traverses a barren and impressive landscape where deserted villages are planted on the sides of dried-up river beds, and where markets and festivals are held, of the sort that we saw in Puerto de Lumbreras. In the pebbles and against the scoured walls of rock we watched the men, women and children in their best and brightest clothes, displaying a love of life that made a vivid contrast with the arid, grey waste of this stony land-scape. A whole section of Spanish life and history was here perceptible in one glance — the Spanish ability to make life, even in the poorest circumstances, into a festival, a ritual that makes one forget one's cares. A festival like this is perhaps just an ordinary village celebration, but it has a style no longer to be found in most other European countries. You can see that the festival is a unique occasion, and that people are conscious of this.

Further on, this dried-up river takes the form of a true canyon. The landscape has much in common, on a small scale, with the Grand Canyon in America. People have hollowed their houses out of caves; a white door marks the entrance to each. One really begins to fancy that one is no longer in Europe. It could be Africa, Asia or South America. Was this the reason why the Spaniards discovered South America rather than North America? The people who live in these caves are for the most part gypsies, *Gitanos*, but they wear the same *poncho* as South Americans do. They sing and dance to drown their misery. They pound the earth with their feet, and heaven and hell with their singing. It is the same in the neighbourhood of Guadix, an old Roman town with a beautiful square surrounded by stately buildings resting on rows of columns. The town is absolutely still, however — the past broods in silence. If you go through the western entrance to the square you arrive nowhere. There is nothing behind but a great, bare, barren, red, yellow and grey landscape of hills and mountains. Water is scarce here, as it is further on in Purullana, a red-coloured village carved out of worn, dry red valleys; the caves that form the villagers' houses are hollowed out of the rock, all of them white-washed, with white chimneys too. It is certainly picturesque, but it is more than that: it is a basic form of human existence. Out of the red caves a shrill nasal voice will sing, triumphantly rousing a dozen echoes, of man's victory his voice exalts him into the self-confident lord of his poverty, into a rich man. This is the secret power not only of gypsies but also of the Spaniards, who took over their songs and dances and converted them from the expression of Slav melancholy into a crude, harsh scream of joy and power.

We arrive now in Granada, a mild and beautiful city built on two hills, the Alhambra and the Albaicin, spurs of the Sierra Nevada, which slope down into a fertile plain traversed by the rivers Genil and Darro. Here more than 160.000 people live in a glorious climate, under u clear blue sky, amid a luxuriant vegetation, at the foot of the snow-capped Sierra Nevada. Granada, whose history dates from 500 AD, is indebted for its prosperity and name to the Moors; they called the city Garnata. After the fall of Córdoba in 1236, Granada became the most important centre of the Moorish kings and enjoyed its greatest fame. It was not only a centre of Arabic culture; the Greek and Roman classics were also studied there. In 1492, mainly as a result of divisions between the Moorish rulers, it fell into the hands of Ferdinand and Isabella, the Catholic Monarchs. The last king but one had fallen in love with a Christian girl called Zoraya ('Morning Star'). Queen Aicha, refusing to accept this managed to depose him and to substitute her only son, Boabdil. He was to be the last of the Moorish rulers. After the fall of his city he was banished by Ferdinand and Isabella; on his way to the south he cast one more glance at the city so dear to him, and sighed. The spot is still called 'Suspiro del Moro' (the Moor's Sigh). But although the Moors were driven out their influence lasted for a long time afterwards, and can still be seen even today in the fierce black eyes of the people of Granada, in the southern distinction of their gestures, and in the architecture of the city. If you stand on the Alhambra hill you can see over the

Alhambra, Granada ▶

city in all directions and enjoy a splendid view of its houses, which are all built round a patio. Life in a house like this is for the most part directed inward. There are few if any windows on to the street, but plenty of light falling on the inner sides. Often the first storey stands on a row of columns, and one can see the womenfolk sitting among them, busy with their household chores.

The *Calat Alhambra* (the Red Castle), usually called just the Alhambra, is the most imposing building that the centuries have bequeathed to Granada, and it still dominates the city today. Originally built in the twelfth century, it was constantly extended during the next four hundred years. It consists of two palaces, those of Mohammed V and Yusef I. It was the residence of many Sultans. You can walk round it for hours, and gradually a beneficent feeling of peace and harmony will come over you from looking at so much symmetry and so much refined and sensitive ornamentation. The Arabic inscriptions form a very special kind of decoration. One naturally visits the Patio de los Leones, the Sala de las Dos Hermanas, the Sala de las Camas (beds), the womens' quarters, the bathrooms, where the sultan's wives bathed, the gardens in which they walked, and then once again the sleeping quarters, in order to test the acoustics. If you stand in one corner and whisper, your companion can hear you in the opposite corner. Thus the women could have no secrets between one another. On your trip a gypsy woman may well ask you if she may read your hand. She does this from a sense of business and of the contents of your wallet, but one must not omit an experience of this sort just because of the money. She reads your whole character from your hand and it may well be that you will find that as she finishes she may keep hold of your hand, lead you to the walls, whence there is an extensive view over the city, and say: 'Look, there the people live with their good luck and their bad luck, with their joy and sorrow, and I know all about all of them.' It does not matter whether all she says is true or not; the point is that it may touch a strange chord which we northerners do not know how to handle, and which can be useful here in opening your eyes and your heart to Granada and all it stands for. You become sentimental! That is the power of Granada, the most romantic city in Spain, where the water murmurs all the time in the Moorish drainage system down from the Alhambra and the Albaicín. An eternal stream, the sound of which accompanies you all the time, like the sound of crickets, and deepens the meaning of everything you see. The Alhambra is graceful, but one can also imagine how here the Moorish rulers in their feuds organized bloodbaths for each other, while the women wailed alone in their quarters or sat quietly waiting for the sultan's call.

Granada has known further blood baths. In the civil war dozens of people were shot here, including the famous poet Garcia Lorca. The Falangists had no time for poets. After the Alhambra we go to the gardens of the Generalife opposite, the gardens of the sultans, with fountains, cypresses, roses and beautiful Arabian summer-houses. A fairy-tale world which you must certainly see. It has been described in words by Arabian poets and also by Garcia Lorca. Away in the distance you may hear guitars and castanets from the Sacro Monte, where the gypsies live and dance. Late at night in their festive costumes they dance for the public in their decorated cave-dwellings. Their only contact with ordered society is through begging or theft of varying kinds, but they had and still have a philosophy about this. They do not cooperate with organized society, for they have felt outcasts since the time when gypsy smiths forged the nails with which Christ was nailed to the cross. That is one legend, but there is also the conviction, born out of years on the steppes, that this kind of life is better than an ordered existence. Their songs testify continually to this nostalgia. Down through the centuries they have maintained their own individuality and character, even with regard to the Spaniards. They are not the original creators of Spanish dancing; they took it over, as they did in other lands, because of their

matchless musical gifts. This people deserves to live mainly because of the way in which, in them, the human body manages to give the illusion of belonging to the earth five feet above it. That is Granada. The Spanish dance, for that is the dance of the gypsies, is a dance in which the whole body from toes to fingers is involved in one great rhythmic happening. It is a liberating dance; five feet above the earth indeed. And if you are lucky enough to find the guitarist, Antonio Albaicín, playing before you the whole evening, somewhere in Granada, then you see how refined the art of guitar-playing is, and how this mostly unwritten music draws its force from variations and modulations on an often well-known theme.

After an evening like that one recalls that Manuel de Falla lived and worked here, and that he and Garcia Lorca produced poetry and music for the people of Granada. Falla lived in a little house with his sister, almost like a monk, frugally and without comfort. If you walk in the early morning, when it is still beautifully cool, through the rarefied air of the streets to see something more of the city, you find before your eyes a white city! A white city with a lot of bustling brown people, with awnings spread out over the narrow streets in front of the cafés against the coming heat of the sun. Even early in the morning many people will be sitting there drinking their coffee, their '103' or 'Pedro Domecq' brandy, or their *manzanilla,* a light sherry. This is a luxury not only to be watched but also to be shared. When one has thus given the day some form, it is time to go and look at the cathedral. It is an immense cathedral with huge interior spaces supported by triple pillars; a cool place for prayer and devotions. The Catholic king, Ferdinand, and Isabella lie buried there, as well as Philip the Fair and Joanna the Mad. Whole golden organs hang there between the pillars — a typical example of Spanish luxury and extravagance — but in this huge space they are hardly at all disturbing. Much is reminiscent of Italian Renaissance architecture. There are statues and paintings by Alonso Cano, Alfonso and Terdro de Nena and other Spaniards, but also by Memlinck, Van der Weyden, Dierick Bouts and Botticelli. In the sacristy one can admire the beautifully embroidered garments of kings and emperors, as well as the crown and sceptre of Ferdinand and many gold and silver cups, rings and tapestries. But over and above all, over and above this history of piety, of pride at the conquest of the Moors, of the Inquisition, wars, blood and tears, reigns the coolness of the ineffable interior. The cathedral was built from 1523 to 1561.

We must now leave Granada. Just like Boabdil, we shall look back in sorrow from the mountain-pass to the south of the city, the Suspiro del Moro, but nevertheless go on, as he did, to Motril. There he had to leave Spain; we follow the coast to Malaga.

Malaga is one of the oldest towns in Spain. It is just the place in which to hibernate. It has everything to make a stay unforgettable. The British found that out years ago. They selected Malaga as a winter resort at the beginning of this century, just as they picked on Nice and Cannes at the same time. And now, as in Nice and Cannes, they are no longer the only ones. Malaga looks like a land of plenty, with oranges, lemons, grapes, melons, bananas, figs and olives in abundance. Perhaps in Malaga you will go to a bull-fight, to see how both men and women become equally enraptured at this battle against the irrational forces of nature, supposedly embodied in the bull, at the elegance of the bull fighters, and at the agility of both man and animal. Rich and poor are present, all in their best clothes, with shoes brightly polished. The rich sit in the shady seats, *sombra,* the poor in the sun, *sol,* and those who are neither rich nor poor sit in the *sol y sombra,* partly in the sun, partly in the shade. The spectators all arrive in good time, for a bull fight is pretty well the only thing in Spain that begins punctually. No one would want to miss even a minute of the spectacle. It is a real national festival which starts with the participants marching in to the blaring, exciting music of the band. They all enter the ring in a fixed sequence: first the two keepers of the bulls on horseback then the three matadors, the men who wage the last battle with the bull and kill him with the sword (*estoque*). They wear splendid clothes embroidered with gold and when they appear the crowd reverently mutters their names. After them come the men with the *banderillas*, who have to plant the darts decorated with ribbons in the bull's neck after the picadors, on horseback, have already weakened the beast's neck. It is a medieval spectacle. The horses are old nags and are often badly knocked about, although they are protected by thick quilts. The picadors go into action just after the bull has been released. If it is a wild, brave animal, one can indeed witness a show in which courage and elegance cause shivers of fear and delight, for it is a dangerous sport, and every torero knows that he is risking his life and playing with death. Death, killing and the elemental ferocity of nature play the dominant and thrilling part in a bull fight, and the fight thus becomes an outlet for human instincts which otherwise could well assume quite a different form of Spanish fury. Sometimes, however, the bulls are not at all pugnacious; the animal stands there watching the performance, looking somewhat bewildered and pitiful, and the proceedings never amount to a real trial of strength. Sometimes, too, the animal is so tormented beforehand by the picadors and banderilleros that its strength is exhausted and it waits resignedly for death. Then the spectators protest violently; they roundly curse the bull, the bull fighters and the management of the bull ring. They demand a fresh bull, and sometimes they get one. As a spectator, you are caught up in the atmosphere of tension and excitement, roused by the music and the shouts of applause from the crowd all round you, so that your northern blood flows more swiftly in your veins, and you perhaps get some idea of the significance which these fights have for the Spaniards. For in origin the bull-fight is a religious festival, the sacrifice of a victim. The bull is 'Mother Nature'; the bull-fighter combats nature and seeks to overcome her. That is how the *aficionados* see this trial of strength. The aficionados are the real

enthusiasts and connoisseurs; they write and talk about a fight as only specialists can, and in addition they are the supporters of the toreros, by no means tender in their criticism but liberal with their applause. The status of the bull-fighter in Spain has always been and still is a high one. Politicians are glad to have him as a friend.

Outside Malaga, in the direction of Gibraltar, are the resorts of Torremolinos, Fuengirola and Marbella, all pearls of the Costa del Sol; once simple fishing villages, they are now real tourist resorts, terribly busy in the summer in particular. In the winter it is still better there.

Spanish is a world language and a very beautiful language; without it, your contact with the country is noticeably restricted, for the Spaniards you are an *estranjero*, a foreigner. People will be polite to you, but each word of Spanish that one speaks opens eyes, ears and hearts. Then the man from Malaga will explain to you: We call our cathedral the *Manquita*, because the second tower was never completed, and Manquita is the diminutive of *mance*, which means a woman with one arm.

In the week before Easter, Holy Week, there are the festivals and processions: fantastic, fairy-tale rituals, more pagan than one might think. Priest, monks, men with Klu Klux Klan hoods on, sinners, thieves, all and sundry take part and help to carry, for example, the Virgin de la Estrella (Our Lady of the Star), the Virgin de la Esperanza (Our Lady of Hope), the Lord Jesus, the Lord Jesus of the gypsies, the Lord Jesus of the disabled, and so on. In Spain there are saints and patrons for everyone. The patron of *butagas* is called Nuestra Senora de las Candelas (Our Lady of the Candles). As a whole, however, it is an impressive spectacle; whether one is a believer or not, one is affected by solemnities which are at the same time very human, for if a member of a procession feels thirsty he will just nip into a café and quickly slake his thirst. The whole think has a primitive beauty and force which often take an ominous form. It will hardly surprise you to hear that less than a hundred years ago ritualised sacred dances were performed before the altars in the cathedrals. For ecstasy is not alien to Spaniards; we are not far distant from primitive blood sacrifices and we stand all the time with one foot in Africa. This side of the Spanish character always comes very much to the fore in mass ceremonies of this sort, including bull-fights and football, and also in the songs and dances. This is an aspect of Spain that makes the Spaniard a different person from the average European. He is still familiar with the essence of what we call, for the sake of convenience, romanticism. The Spaniard, feels himself linked to something that amounts to more than the wretchedness of daily existence. For centuries he built up a stamping dance over death. He wants life, sees it as greater than it is, and thus makes it greater. Through this alone the daily life of the Spaniard has gained colour and content; it is less grey and boring than life elsewhere. Although a man may go to church no longer, there slumbers in him a sort of religious instinct that is the source of all the turbulence and movement in the life and history of the Spaniards. Read Unamuno, Ortega y Casset, Lorca and many others, and you will acquire a better understanding of what I am trying to say here in far too small a space and in far too few words. In Spain there reigns a power that makes people more human and sensitive to aspects of life which many of us have buried under a daily routine of work that encloses our feelings like a suit of armour. In Spain people still know what to do with the night, because the dividing line was never drawn so rigorously, because the Spaniards have the time for it; their lives are not yet ruled by the clock. They find nothing more difficult than to arrive on time, and they always have the most charming smiles and excuses ready when they are late. And I believe that this attitude of the Spaniards will last a long time yet, although in the end every nation will probably yield, for lack of any other plan, to the advantages and disadvantages of Americanization.

Now on to Ronda, which is surrounded by mountains,

situated on a plateau and cleft by a chasm which splits the town into two parts connected by a bridge. The scenery round the town is fascinating in its quiet beauty. A town like this, one thinks to oneself, will probably last forever, for it is embedded in these indestructible mountains and almost forms part of them. The cleft (in Spanish, *tajo,* that runs through the middle of the town is a curious freak of nature, in which the water from the mountains foams and roars — a grandiose spectacle. Little streets lead down to the bottom. The left bank of the tajo shelters the oldest part of Ronda, which is a romantic town with narrow, winding streets and a large number of small cafés. And it can happen, as so often in Spain, at any rate if you speak a little bit of Spanish, that a man will take you into the town in the evening, show you everything, offer you a drink, tell you that he is alone and delighted to have your company, and offer you a splendid evening. You will think that this is nonsense. That could well be so, but ten to one it is not, and you can happily accept his invitation, at any rate if you are not a woman on your own. Then he will take you to places where there is dancing and a good guitarist is playing, either among gypsies or Spaniards, and it will be the evening of your life, for the dancing and playing will be really good. Your evening will be completely organized and yet give the impression of spontaneity, for Spaniards leave no part of their leisure empty; they fill it up with heartiness and pride and make passionate use of every minute of it. It was the Spanish philosopher, Salvador Madariaga, who once said that so long as the ideal of the modern state was the bank building and a well functioning banking system the Spaniard would have little to contribute to the development of our modern world. He has always though that trade is beneath his dignity, or at any rate that it is not the only path to human happiness, to a 'heroic existence'.

Naturally this is a generalization. There are plenty of crafty Spanish business men, but even they have something about them that is almost an exuse for their attitude.

33.   Donkeys carry everything, even sugar-cane

34.   The grain is threshed with rod and clapper

35.   A square, typical of many villages round Madrid

36.   Gibraltar, the most southerly and most disputed point of Spain

37.   Cádiz, a white city

38.   Fans for sale in Seville
39.   The old quarter of Santa Cruz in Seville ▶

40.   The Giralda Tower in Seville

41. A traffic policeman watches over the entrance to the Puerta
de Perdón

42.   Wall of the mosque ('Mesquita') in Córdoba

43.   'My mosque shall be a forest of palms... (Córdoba)

44. The castle of Belmonte, one of the many strongholds in Castile

45. It was against these mills in La Mancha that Don Quixote and Sancho Panza fought

47. The centre of Madrid — the heart of Spain
46. The flowers in the Plaza de España in Madrid are watered
    every day

48.   In the Prado one sees many people copying the masterpieces

FROM SOUTHERN SPAIN TO MADRID

One can naturally leave southern Spain by going from Algeciras to Spanish Morocco; one can also leave it, but less completely, by going to Gibraltar, the town that is still in British hands, a circumstance which is often a thorn in the flesh of the Spaniards. It certainly was and is used as a thorn by the Spanish government in order to distract attention from less attractive internal questions.

First, then, to Cádiz, one of Spain's oldest ports. Phoenicians, Greeks, Romans and Moors all lived in this city, and in struggles lasting years made it what it is now. Excavations have been carried out, and among the finds were Egyptian amulets and Roman sarcophagi. The Normans plundered the city and laid it waste. In 1262 Alfonso the Wise reconquered it for the Spaniards. The poet, Byron, sang of it in *Childe Harold*. It is a port with a glorious climate, beautifully situated on a small peninsula, white against the deep blue sky and the very green sea. The salt pans lie steaming, and the mountains of salt glisten under the hot sun. The city possesses many parks and *paseos* (avenues), such as the Alameda de Apodaca and the Parque Genores. A beautiful old quarter is La Vina. The centre of the city is the Plaza de Constitución. The cathadral dates from the seventeenth century and holds the remains of the composer, Manuel de Falla. Not far from Cádiz, off Cape Trafalgar, Nelson met his death. One must visit the Iglesia de Capuchinos (Capuchin Church) to see the pictures by Murillo that hang there, and the Museo de Bellas Artes for the works by Zurbaran. It is a city full of the history and mysterious life of every age. Make the time to share its life. In days gone by the girl dancers of Cádiz were famous, and one can still find cafés where their dancers are performed.

On the way from Cádiz to Seville we pass through Jerez de la Frontera, a rich and fertile spot, with orange trees and palms, and balconies full of flowers. But the wine cellars, (*bodegas*), are the town's greatest attraction. Those of Pedro Domecq, Gonzalez Byass, the Marques del Merito and Williams and Humbert are the best known; they are famous all over the world. Go into one of them and have a glass of sherry, young, old, very old or still older; a whole world will open up before you, perhaps a cloudy one, for sherry is a stiff drink. You float five feet above the ground, and the inhabitants of Jerez, old sherry men, who know all about sherry and its effect on the human spirit, watch you with a gentle smile and lend a willing ear to all the assertions that suddenly spring to your lips. They know that eternity sits deep, and that once the wine reaches the spirit it does not so much speak as stir gently under the human words that hang round it like a cloak. And now we move on along the valley of the Guadalquivir to Seville, a city of about half a million inhabitants and, with Granada, one of the pearls of Andalusia, Al-Andalus as the Moors called it, a luxuriant garden of high culture.

One enters Seville through the old quarter of Triana, named after Trajan, the Roman emperor, who was a Spaniard by birth. Then comes the bridge over the Guadalquivir, which is very wide here and kept deep by dredgers, as a result of which Seville is still an important seaport.

Over the bridge to the left lie the docks, and to the right, adjoining the Paseo de Cristobal Colon, where the Torre del Oro (Golden Tower) built by the Moors stands, the Paseo de las Delicias (of Delights). Delights indeed! A little further on lies the Maria Luisa park, with its palms, fountains and palaces, where it is pleasant to sit in the shade in the morning, with a sherry or a cup of strong coffee in front of you. One can also be driven round it in a little carriage.

The centre of the city is dominated by the huge cathedral with its Moorish tower, the Giralda, once the minaret from which Mohammedans were called to the mosque, which stood where the cathedral now stands. We will not go into the cathedral straight away; we must look for a hotel. Naturally there are always the expensive ones, such as the Hotel Alfonso XIII, but we want something different. Fortunately our shoes are grey from the dust and the shoe-shine man is always in the neighbourhood. While he is carefully polishing your shoes, apparently so that the shine will last forever, he will tell you to find a simple hotel, a hotel for Spaniards. That was how we found one: The Venezia Hotel, a small old mansion in the Plaza del Duque de la Victoria, a square with palms and carriages, drowsy coachmen and somewhat more active taxi drivers, right in the heart of the city. One has so far seen little of the city, but already one feels overcome by the pleasant indolence affected so stylishly by the citizens of Seville. It reeks of strange festivals, and it is indeed the city of *fiestas* and *ferias* par excellence.

Ferias, tradition, aristocratic spirit, a mild climate in winter and summer, colours, historical buildings, white houses, patios alive with flowers and Sevillians, old palaces the colour of ochre, that is Seville. Alfonse X, nicknamed 'the

Wise', who ruled in the second half of the thirteenth century, gave the city as a reward for its loyalty the following motto: *'Muy noble, muy leal, muy heroica y invencible'* (very noble, noble, very loyal, very heroic, and invincible).

The Alcazar, the old palace of the Almohades, was enlarged b the Christian princes, especially by Pedro el Cruel (the Cruel). He took into his service Moorish architects who had been converted to Christianity. And although the Alcazar did not become such a disciplined and harmonious marvel as the Alhambra at Granada, one must go to see this conglomeration of palaces in many different styles, and the beautiful gardens. The various sections all contradict each other, yet in some wonderful way they have merged into a unity which is surprising in its combination of Eastern and European architectural styles. It is really not so much a combination as a harmonious mixture. What is the point of strictness and discipline in Seville? It is Andalusia at its best. The light, the sun and the airy mode of life span eveything — turbulent hitory and strange life of today. Wonders seem to fill the streets.

Through the courtyard of orange trees one finally enters the cathedral, after already passing through the 'Door of Forgiveness'. Then comes the vast, cool interior of the cathedral itself, where everything is redolent of history, kings, noblemen and conquistadores, the conquerors of South America. One sees the wealth piled up in church treasures, the great pictures of Murillo, Zurbaran, el Greco and Goya. One sees the four strong virgins, as high as houses, that support the heavy tomb of Columbus, carrying him through the centuries. One can spend hours here. The middle of the day is the best time. When the streets are quivering with heat it is cool in this cathedral.

When one emerges again one blinks in the fierce sunlight. One just stands still and feels oneself becoming one with the gently throbbing meditative unity of Seville. Do I exaggerate? No, I can see the blind, the beggars and the poor. They are still there all the time. And yet they look less pitiable. And so they are. They are pitied less and seen rather as disabled people. Well, then: a crooked arm or leg? An arm or a leg is not a whole man. Thus they always look more independent, and they feel more independent too. They have breeding and they are astute.

Arriving at the Ayuntamento (town hall), we strike off to the right into the Calle de las Sierpes, the Bond Street of Seville, roofed with awnings against the sun. There are also some excellent restaurants in it. Further on there are the gentlemen's clubs, where men sit in heavy leather armchairs, smoking, chatting and reading their newspapers. In Holy Week Seville is a sparkling mass of colour, a parade of proud men and woman on horseback, with magnificent processions in which all the treasures of the churches are carried — decorated madonnas and so on; it is, in short, a Spanish festival. But you may meet a sombre man who stands watching the spectacle with a critical and surly look. He will have a finely-cut face and look like a scholar or a poet. Seeing you laughing, he will shake his head sadly as he addresses you: 'To be sure, this all looks beautiful to you. It is something different from what you see in your own land. It could be beautiful, too. But it is idle show, the movable scenery of Spain hiding our weaknesses and backwardness; behind it our people lies hungering — not for bread alone, but for jusice and education. This, Señor, is the façade, behind which we lie as dry and uncultivated as the wildernesses of Estremadura. Our hunger for books, culture and education must be stilled if we are to still all the hunger for bread that will follow. With intelligence and faith, Señor. Books and food, that must be the watchword. I am fond of Spain, like Francisco Giner, who got us moving and wanted Spain to hold its cultural position in the world. We want a modern and active life, a life within the best traditions of our people, but not stifled by traditions, in dead forms. Once again I say, books and bread. We have no time for the pious romantic philistinism that calls illiteracy and analphabetism a state of primitive grace. We were on the right road, but the revolution interrupted the work, the work of men like the philosophers Unamuno and Ortega y Gasset, the writer Pio Baroja, the poets Ramon del Valle Inclan, Garcia Lorca and Machado. Then there were our composers, Albeniz, Granados and Manuel de Falla. Ah, Señor, our people is a fine people, and it is a question of the spirit of this people and of the tendency to rest that lies deep down in it ... but it should not want to rest now, Señor; it is rusting.'

The speaker was a somewhat older man, who had lived through the revolution and the period that preceded it, when the Republic was indeed taking new paths and was trying, wherever it could with the few means at its disposal, to put the people on its feet and to get it moving in the field of culture. He felt nostalgic for that time. But the young Spaniards of today, especially the students, pay homage to the same ideals. They live in the midst of this age with all its possibilities and they want Spain to play its part in Europe in the economic and cultural fields as well as in that of tourism. Students and artists are demanding more openly the freedom of speech and action on which such co-operation must be based.

In the evening we can go into the ancient quarter of Santa Cruz, a typical old section of the city with a very Eastern look, Quick tongues and intelligent glances surround you in the cafés. Wine, brandy, absinthe, sherry, Malaga — everything you can think of is drunk there, and a great deal of talking is done. There is always an animated atmosphere in a café of this sort, and the words *hombre* (man) and *mujer* (woman) are frequently used. One strolls through the dimly lit streets, still white because of the white walls of the houses, and one sees the slumbering patios, where the flowers are drooping, patios of both rich and poor. Usually the beautiful wrought-iron gates stand open. In the distance you can hear singing, shrill nasal voices pierce you to the very marrow; flamenco is in full swing, there are gay sounds of revelry, and it can last for along time. You may well get drunk. The Spaniard will tolerate this in you, but not in himself, for he regards the loss of control over his passions as an affront to his humanity, his *humanidad*. You will meet very few drunken Spaniards. On the other hand, nothing human is alien to him, and so it may well happen that you find yourself sauntering late at night through the narrow streets, arm in arm with a man unknown to you a few hours ago, who quotes softly — or even quite loud — from a play by Calderon de la Barca:

Que es la vida? Un frenesi.
(What is life? Mere madness.)
Que es la vida? Una ilusión.
(What is life? An illusion.)
Una sombra, una ficción
(A shadow, a fiction)
Toda la vida es sueño
Y los sueños sueño son.
(All life is a dream
And dreams are a dream.)

Next day you should return to this quarter once more and discover the little church of La Macarena, with its beautiful statue of Our Lady before an altar radiant with gold, paid for, so they say, by the gold of the toreros, who come here to pray before they go to fight. It is almost superfluous to add that Seville has a beautiful Plaza de Toros. There is a curious old tobacco factory there too; it looks like an old palace. Seville is a incomprehensible city, to which one always wants to return; inexhaustible in its rich past, which still paves the streets of today.

Then on to Córdoba. This town was named by the Phoenicians after an old olive oil mill or press, which was known as a *corteb*. The Moors turned this into *Corthobah*. In 785 Abd el Rahman, the Emir of the caliphate, bought the Christian church of St. Vincent in order to build a mosque, a mosque so impressive in design and size, that only the one at Mecca can be compared with it. He erected the 850 pillars, the forest of palms, with the main entrance facing Mecca, and outside the mosque he laid out a garden with orange trees, There was an entrance to the mosque at the end of each row of pillars, and it was the Emir's intention that the faithful should go straight on from the orange grove into the colonnades of the mosque — after taking off their shoes, of course.

Alas, after the Reconquista, to which Córdoba too·fell a victim in 1236, the palm forest was desecrated by the Christians, who turned it into a cathedral. And what had once been open and light, so that the faithful could see Mecca as they lay in prayer and their gaze meet the prophet Mohammed, was darkened and covered up by the Christians. But the *Mezquita* is still a sight worth seeing. It formed the centre of a luxurious city without equal in its time. Abd el Rahman came with some Moorish soldiers, who married Spanish woman, and after a few battles there was less and less Moorish blood in the veins of the inhabitants. A new race was born, one might say, but a race that lived and throught in a completely Moorish way. The people washed themselves a great deal. There were hundreds of bath-houses all over the city, which also contained a large number of smaller mosques. The people were skilled leather-workers and also made beautifully chased objects of gold and silver, and these arts live on in Córdoba today.

Like every people familiar with the desert, the Moors knew the value of water. It was they who, all over the south of Spain and as far north as they penetrated, laid out extensive irrigation systems and promulgated laws against wasting water or neglecting the irrigation works. Under their rule Spain became once again what it had been for the Romans, the granary of Europe. It is a pity that after conquering the Moors the Christians, out of short-sighted religious zeal, either destroyed these irrigation systems or allowed them to fall into disrepair.

In the time when the Moors made Córdoba into one of the most prosperous cities in Europe four languages were spoken there: classical Arabic, the language of the Koran and the intellectuals; a variety of Arabic for daily use; the Church Latin of the Middle Ages; and a Roman dialect derived from Latin and spoken by the ordinary man. This dialect was one day to become Spanish. Well-being, wealth, luxury and, on the whole, peace prevailed. People were tolerant towards each other. Arabic scholars and philosophers worked alongside Spanish ones. Averroes, a Spanish Mohammedan, translated the works of Aristotle, although the latter had produced books that Moors were officially forbidden to read. Averroes behaved like a Greek philosopher; he did not remain sitting behind his lectern, but travelled all over the country in order to publicize his theses. Thanks to the toleration that prevailed, he was able to do this. Maimonides too, a Jewish scholar and a precursor of Spinoza, was able to publish his opinions freely, although they were in opposition to the Koran. The Catholic Monarchs took a different view of these matters; they commanded all Mohammedan Spaniards to leave the country, and the Jews had to go too.

At last, after wandering through the city, which still retains traces of its great past, we take a seat outside a café. There you may be addressed by a young man called Enrique Francisco Maria Soler, who in a sly, polished and unassuming way crosses your path where the tourist must be addressed and tempted, namely, outside a café. He approaches with a surprised smile, takes a seat, offers you a drink, speaks fluent French, of which he is proud, and tells you various things about his city, of which he is also proud. He asks you if you have got a hotel and offers to take you to a good, cheap one. He does so, too, and wants no money. He gets that from the proprieter. He will also call for you in the evening and take you to a spot where there are flamenco singers and dancers who will sing for you. At the most, Enrique will accept a drink; he will even offer you drinks, and still take no money. He gets that from the boss or lady who runs the house for girls of easy virtue where he will also gladly take you, if you want that. That is simply his profession. He puts on an act of elegance and polish like a gently sauntering robber knight.

But at any rate you roam through Córdoba and hear guitar music. You come to a halt in the late afternoon and life suddenly threatens to acquire a frightening perfection. At a moment like that it is dead quiet, and at just such a moment, *a las cinco de la tarde* (at five o'clock in the afternoon), just on the stroke of five, the greatest torero of al time, Manolete, was tossed on a bull's horns, and his blood and the animal's together stained the sand red. He died, and he is buried here in Córdoba.

About seven o'clock in the evening you must go, along with all the inhabitants of Córdoba, to the informal parade that all Spaniards hold about that time in every town, in every village or hamlet. Young and old, men, women and children have all left their houses and are walking up and down their boulevard, greeting each other and talking to each other. This lasts an hour or two, then the women and girls go home to prepare the meal, which is served about ten or half-past. The men gather in the meantime in their cafés.

We leave now for Madrid, still following the Guadalquivir for a little way as far as Bailen, where a pleasant *albergue* (inn), that of San José, invites us to have a meal. It is a sort of big farm. One can also go on to Ubeda, where a *parador* (a state-run hotel) has been installed in the old palace of Ortega Cambrio. Ubeda is a fine town, an architectural marvel, like nearby Baeza. Then on northward to Valdepeñas, which lies amid vineyards in New Castile. Still further north we enter la Mancha, where the windmills and the men on horses and donkeys continually remind you of Don Quixote and Sancho Panza. It is a land of white villages on endless plateaux. Go into one, as we did. There was a café full of people waiting for the bus. People wait a lot in Spain and quite enjoy it. The proprieter came to serve us and we saw the little brown saucers of sizzling fried shrimps which the people round us were eating. Our look alone was sufficient to decide the proprieter to offer us these sizzling dishes. They were excellent: shrimps fried in oil and garlic. We sat there for hours and began to understand why it is really not a bad thing to have to wait for a bus or train in Spain. It never leads to panic, but to a sort of holiday mood.

About thirty miles from Madrid we pass through Aranjuez, with its beautiful gardens on the bank of the River Tagus. The huge royal palace was the summer residence of Isabella of Castile. It was later enlarged by Philip II and succeeding kings.

On a tributary of the Tagus, the Manzanares, lies Madrid, known as *Majerit* by the Moors; it was not much more than a fort in those days. Now it is the capital of Spain, with over two million inhabitants. The wide main street, the Gran Via, is still crowded far into the night. The cafés stay open for a long time, although the government has fixed the time for shutting at one o'clock in the morning, so that the citizens of Madrid, the Madrileños, who are known as *gatos* (cats), can get to work on time a little more easily. Madrid is a university city and the centre of the intellectual and spiritual life of Spain. It is also a centre of brooding discontent, one more burden for the Franco régime. There simmers in the city a desire for freedom and cooperation with Europe that can no longer be suppressed.

Everything begins and ends in the Puerta del Sol, an open space, oval in shape, into which many streets lead and lined with cafés and department stores. The old centre of the city, however, was the Plaza Mayor, where in days gone by the bull-fights were also held. Close by is the Rastro, Madrid's flea-market, where you must go and plunge into a heaving sea of people: lookers-on, buyers, sellers, who always know how to praise their wares in a bizarre and original way. It will cost you a morning, but it will be an unforgettable one; and when later you go to the Prado, the national museum of Spain, and look at the Goyas there, you will see them again, these Spaniards, in the hallucinatory vision of Spain's greatest painter, a farmer's boy from Aragon who went through life armed with a sketchbook in which he recorded everything he saw and who penetrated to the highest court circles. Typical examples of his art are his *Tauromachia,* a series of drawings of bull-fights, and his *Los Desastres de la Guerra,* drawings of the horrors of war. The model for his *Maja Clothed* and *Maja Naked* was no less a person than the Duchess of Alba. Goya has left us a detailed survey of all the turbulent, cruel sweet, earthy life of the Spaniards of his time. Of course, you will see works by other painters in the Prado: Hieronymus Bosch, Van Dyck, Velazquez, El Greco, Zurbaran and others too numerous to mention.

Behind the Prado lies the Parque del Retiro, once intended for princes and princesses, but now the property of all Madrid; there one can still see nursemaids in white aprons walking with the pretty children of the rich, and old ladies being driven round in open carriages — a *fin de siècle* flower that belongs to a bygone age.

But Madrid is also a metropolis. Towards six o'clock the traffic races or stands still as it does in any other city. You can also still see here a fully laden donkey making its way between the shining cars, and you may have to wait on the bridge leading to Toledo for a flock of sheep, which graze on the banks of the Manzanares.

Above all, go and visit the quarter which lies between the Calle de la Cruz, the Calle de San Jeronimo and the Calle del Prado, a triangle full of little pubs where many citizens of Madrid gather towards five o'clock. It's a lively district, where rich and poor crowd together and eat their *gambas* (fried shrimps), their *higados* (pieces of liver), their anchovies and all kinds of other things, naturally aways with a glass of wine — red, white or rosé.

The post office is in the Plaza de la Cibeles. In front of the Cortes, the Spanish parliament building, which is usually closed, you may find a man lying asleep between the lions that flank the entrance. Worth a visit too are the royal palace, (Palacio Real) and the grandiose set of buildings of the Ciudad Universitaria (University) where the best chance of making Spain a modern state probably lies. If you come back late at night to your hotel or boarding-house you may find the doors closed. But don't worry; just start clapping your hands vigorously and before long a man with a stick will appear. He is *el sereno* (the night watchman) and he will have a big bunch of keys with which to open doors.

Pay a visit as well to the streets to the right and left of the Gran Via. They are the throbbing heart of this city, itself the heart of Spain, and it is cheaper there than in the Gran Via itself. Madrid is full of intimate little squares, such as the Plaza Santa Ana and others in the Rastro district. In the centre of the city, too there are many restaurants, both big and small, where one can obtain an excellent meal. In a word, Madrid is a city where there is no need to be bored for a minute.

Don Quixote and Sancho Panza

ESTREMADURA AND THE NORTH-WEST

When we left Seville we could also have taken a more westerly route to the north, through Mérida, Cáceres, Trujillo and Guadalupe. We should then have traversed Estremadura, a region full of strange vistas. It is extremely dry and extremely poor, eaten bare by great flocks of sheep and goats. Here life was, and still is, by no means comfortable. The battle for their daily bread makes the people old, but it does not break their character. They are proud people, often clothed in rags, but they earn their crust of bread with the pride of the conquistadores. Already in days gone by this land drove its inhabitants to seek adventure. Young men with pluck and imagination marched off into the world. It is thus no surprise to find that almost all the conquerors of South America came from Estremadura: Hermán Cortés, Vasco Nuñez de Balboa, Francisco Pizarro, to name only three.

On our way to the north we pass through Mérida, founded by the Romans in the time of the emperor Augustus. We enter the town across the old Roman bridge, which dates from before the Christian era. There is also a Roman stadium, a Roman theatre and in addition, across the bridge to the right, a Moorish castle.

We arrive next in Cáceres, which was originally Celtic and was then conquered by the Romans, who left clear traces behind them, as the Moors did later. Today the town makes a decidedly medieval impression, but you may meet there Don Antonio, who feels lonely, because his wife has gone off to La Coruña in the north and he has to look after himself — a situation which he probably once longed for, but not quite in this way. He would rather have her at home, for now that he is free to do whatever he likes he does not find this freedom so pleasant. He is melancholy, and that makes him generous. He wants to have your company the whole evening and is willing to pay for it. He takes you to a restaurant, treats you to a flamenco singer and goes with you to a night-club; he may even want something more, and he will suggest that to you too. At the end of it all you will have had an evening in Spain that you will remember for a long time.

Next day, have a coffee with brandy in it in the fine Plaza Mayor of Trujillo, the old Turris Julia of the Romans. The square is surrounded by splendid old houses. Pizarro, the conqueror of Peru, was born here. The storks are fond of Trujillo; they nest here in hundreds. Naturally they also build their nests in the huge Moorish castle just outside the town.

One could drive straight on to Madrid from here, but a detour to Guadalupe is well worth the trouble. On the slopes of the Sierra de Guadalupe stands the monastery of Santa Maria de Guadalupe, an old place of pilgrimage for Christians. This is the legend: there was once a cowherd and he lost a cow. After three days he found it dead under a blackberry bush. He drew his knife with the intention of skinning the beast and of taking the valuable hide home with him, but suddenly the cow stood up. The farmer started back in fear, for above it, between the animal's horns, he could see the Virgin Mary. She spoke to him and said that under the blackberry bush an image of herself was hidden. The farmer fled and told the priests of his village

103

what had happened. The priests went to the bush, dug under it and found the image, together with the instruction to build a monastery. And so this monastery was built. You can stay in it yourself. Thanks to be the conquistadores the name Guadalupe occurs often in Central and South America.

We proceed now via Madrid to Toledo, the city of the painter El Greco, whose house still stands there and should certainly be visited. You may perhaps enter the city through the Puerta del Sol, the Sun Gate, with its horse-shoe-shaped opening in the Moorish style. Above the gate stand these words: 'I am the most beautiful and best preserved gate of the city. The Moors built me eight centuries ago and made the entrance like the hooves of their horses. Kings fortified me, and the sun loves and cherishes me: it kisses me every morning in greeting and every evening in parting, and that is why I am called the Puerta del Sol.'

Toledo lies on a high, steep hill in a bend of the Tagus, which flows round the bottom of the hill. Inaccessible and walled round, it was once the seat of Spanish kings and a bulwark against the Moors. However, in 711 they captured the city from the last king of the Visigoths, who are still recalled by the Visagra gate. The Arabs made the city very prosperous, with Moors and Jews living side by side. The lively little citizens of Toledo too, with their brilliant brown eyes, quick gestures and unsurpassed commercial spirit, make you fancy even today that you are in an Eastern town. There was little room on this steep hill, so the streets are narrow and the little squares intimate. The centre of the city is the Plaza Zocodover, where in the evening you can see the citizens of Toledo gather.

In Toledo you have to step over the heads of children! You will have to do this to reach the great cathedral. There is an altar in it with paintings by Goya and El Greco. In Santo Tomé you can see the latter's *Burial of the Count of Orgaz*, one of the most beautiful works of this Greek citizen of Toledo. In the evening you must leave the city and take

49.   The Alcázar of Segovia floats like a ship in space

50. This Roman aquaduct is half a mile long; its stonework is
unpointed

51.   Landscape in Andalusia

52. This Roman theatre in Merida is one of the many Roman remains in Spain
53. The richly ornamented entrance of the College of St Gregory in Valladolid
54/55. At the foot of the old royal city of Toledo flows the Tagus

56. A section of bare landscape in Estremadura

57. Salamanca on the river Tormes with its cathedral and university

58. In contrast with the dry south, one of the luxuriant river valleys in the north

59. A striking sight in La Coruña; the splendid houses with glass verandas ('miradores') by the harbour

60. Santillana del Mar, a typical Basque village; the animals live
downstairs and their owners on the floors above

61.   The Bay of Biscay at Zarauz, a well-known resort

62. Orio, a typical little fishing port in the Basque region

63. Basque dances in a square at Ondarroa
64. The mountains of the Picos de Europa rise steeply near ▶
     Lebana

the road round to the other side of the Tagus, so as to see the city silhouetted against the sky in the twilight. The walls of the Alcázar, badly damaged in the civil war but now restored, stand out in the gloom. Look at the site of Toledo, and I'll wager that a slight shiver runs down your spine, for there is something terrible about the spectacle; something great, too, in the fact that man has succeeded in building a city like this on such a small and inaccessible spot.

The citizens of Toledo are good craftsmen too; Toledo gold and steel work is famous.

We then strike northward, via Madrid, over the Sierra Guadarrama, but not until we have paid a visit to the Escorial, or rather the monastery of San Lorenzo del Escorial, an inaccessible block of grey granite set in a grandiose landscape at the instigation of Philip II. The architect was Juan de Herrera. Before Philip this was the kingdom of the dead, but for twenty-two years he personally led and watched over the building operations.

In the evening the landscape disappears in the huge shadows of the mountains. Philip is filled with a strange gladness. His creation, too disappears in the darkness and sinks into the night against the glowing mountains created by his God. It was to be a compelling symbol for his people of the greatness of their kings and the world empire of Spain. Philip spent much time there. In the last years of his life, harassed by a dreadful illness, he lingered here in horrible, desolate loneliness. He lay in bed, signing his state documents, in a room with a panel in the wall which could be opened during Mass, so that he could see the altar. All the kings were to be buried here. He himself was the first, and before his death he commanded that people should pray for his soul for centuries: 'for,' he said, 'even the ordinary man sins a great deal; how many more sins must be committed by a man who is called to rule over an empire.'

We go on further north, into Castile, the land of castles,

of which Spain has many. One of them stands in Segovia at a spot where two rivers meet, the Eresma and the Clamores. The country round about is rugged and wild. The king's castle, the Alcázar, stands out at the head of the town, and the cathedral with its solid tower lies behind; after that the rest of the town slopes down to the lower part, where the huge Roman aqueduct runs across a fine old square. This aqueduct, the best preserved example in existence, is 880 yards long and has 148 arches, some of them 90 feet high; it is still used to supply water today. There is always a tremendous bustle in the square, in the cafés and in Juan Bravo street, which runs from here to the cathedral. It is a sociable street, with plenty of bars, where you can eat and drink all the specialities of Spain; but you will also see there many old palaces worthy of a royal city. One can spend a peaceful day here looking at the cathedral and the Romanesque churches, and walking along the Ronda de Lucia and the Paseo de la Alameda, where the El Parral monastery stands. Later, in the evening, you can sit down in Azoguejo Square, outside one of the many cafés. The atmosphere is a more northern one than in Toledo, but just as lively. Sheep, donkeys, people and modern traffic mingle noisily with each other. You must also go to see the Casa de los Picos. Once upon a time over 100.000 people lived in Segovia — there are fewer than 40.000 today.

As I have already said, Spain is the land of castles, some of them lonely ones, like that of Coca, built of brick, a huge, red pile, or those of Cuellar, Sepulveda and Pedraza. Sometimes the whole city is a fortress, like Avila, encircled by a wall with eighty towers. The full name of the city is Avila de los Caballeros, Avila of the Knights. It is an austere, grey city, a huge mass of stone, built by man against his fellow-men; a pious Castilian city too, a city 'of stones and saints', as the saying goes, where the great mystic, Teresa of Avila, was born, lived and worked, influencing the whole of Spain. She regulated the lives of

Avila

nuns in convents for centuries. Her statue stands here in Avila in the square named after her. She was a mystic, but also a very practical person.

When the city was captured from the Moors it had to be re-peopled. Men and women were brought from Asturias, and it was their northern spirit that rebuilt the city, with its twenty and more churches and many monasteries. It is a medieval city.

Now on to Salamanca, the oldest university city of Spain, where all the great ones of the land send their sons to study. Salamanca became rich and great through its scholars. It is a monumental city, with its splendid cathedrals — the old one and the 'new' one (which dates from 1500). It was those days that saw the start of the great resurgence of the Catholic Church, the Counter-Reformation. Earnest men and women like St. Teresa brought a deepening of faith and a new conquest of the world through the pursuit of learning, the stimulation of art, the encouragement of a sober life. Fray Luis de Leon wrote a splendid book, *The Names of Christ*. In it he explains the various names

given to Christ in the Bible. First he gives a literal rendering of the word and then the various meanings which that word had in the original society in which it was used. His lectures were a model of how a Christian and a scholar could use language in such a way that the Inquisitor could not lay a finger on him; yet he said what he wanted to say, and his lectures made him the talk of Spain. If he were alive now, he would see that today as well there are men all over Spain who know how to keep their country's name high in the very same way and in much the same circumstances, that is, under a régime that regards the free expression of opinion as a threat to the state.

The Castilian landscape is a severe and sober one, and it has always produced severe and sober men and women, generally with a pronounced will of their own. Everywhere here you will find unity and harmony, wisdom and realism. The university was in Salamanca, but the soil that nourished it was Castile, through which you are driving and where every village has its surprises and its history.

The province of Salamanca is midway between north and south. There are beautiful villages to be seen there, such as Ledesma, Béjar and Candelario, and the old city of Ciudad Rodrigo, with its fine twelfth-century cathedral. The vine still grows luxuriantly here. The peasants are tawny and taller than in the south, but their eyes are not so black and glittering. They are not so exuberant, they live more modestly, and they are inclined to wait to see which way the cat is going to jump. However, a few words of Spanish from your lips will soon loosen their tongues.

Then we approach Valladolid, the Balad Walid (the territory of Walid) as the Moors called it. From the thirteenth century onwards Valladolid was the residence of the kings of Castile. In the Semana Santa (Holy Week) there are the most splendid processions to be seen here, no whit inferior in colourfulness to those of Seville, but more sober and stately. It is an old city, with beautiful buildings, inhabited in earlier days by aristocratic and wealthy people who have left their mark on it. Just before Valladolid you pass through Tordesillas; it was in the palace of this city on the River Duero that Joanna the Mad, the daughter of Ferdinand and Isabella, was finally shut up for the rest of her life, mainly to prevent her from making good her claim to the throne and to separata her for good from Philip the Fair, who had little feeling for kingship and plenty for feasting; he was hostile to the austere Spanish spirit. As we go further north-west it may get colder and more inhospitable because of the wild mountain-ranges, but the people remain hot-blooded and their *fiestas* are as colourful as those of the south. One drives through a huge, strange landscape. Seldom have I seen anything so impressive as the Picos de Europa, the highest peaks in this Cantabrian coastal range. One can ski, indulging in winter sports there to one's heart's content, and if you are fond of mountain-climbing you can do that too. The whole north-west of Spain is largely neglected by tourists, who all speed south as fast as they can in search of the sun, yet it is a beautiful region, with beautiful towns and villages and attractive people. I once rambled along the coast from the luxury resort of San Sebastian where the rulers of Spain spend the summer because it is too hot in Madrid to La Coruña, and from there southward to Vigo and the Portuguese frontier. The ports and fishing villages are unique. The harbours are for the most part natural inlets in the coast, like Bilbao and Santander; the fishing villages lie on little bays and are all beautifully situated. It is a good region for holidays. You will meet the Basques, the people from austere Asturias and the Galicians. You can eat dozens of different kinds of fish, both sea-water and freshwater. The latter are caught in the hundreds of streams that flow down to the sea from the mountains. The fishing is marvellous. We were once in one of these fishing villages about two o'clock in the afternoon. We did not want a full meal and went into an ordinary café. We began with a glass of wine at the bar and asked the proprieter if he had anything to eat. No, he replied, only a few olives. Meanwhile we carried on drinking the wine, a cold, white wine.

No, he hadn't anything to eat, he said, but he had a white cat and a parrot. He was an animal lover; he had also had a dog, but that had died. But the cat and the parrot got on very well together. To prove this, he let the parrot out of its cage and put it on the table, and then the cat next to it. They certainly were quite friendly towards each other. We expressed our admiration and made to go. However, he signed to us to wait, and we heard something sizzling in the kitchen. A moment later his wife came proudly in with a plateful of fried fish. He wouldn't let us pay.

And so we came to Betanzos, with its silted-up harbour, whence part of the Armada set sail. We sat down in the village square under the arcades, opposite the little white church and the white houses, all with the big glass conservatories characteristic of this region. It may well happen that a man will break away from the group and suddenly say hard things about life and society, and that the best thing you can do is to go into the mountains and live in a cave, for nothing is worth while. This is not simply an attack on the government; his complaint is more general. He wants to be free, free even of this village, which is itself pretty remote. He wants to be quite alone and independent. There is something in a man like this that is common to many Spaniards, especially in the north. They do not want to carry the burden of the world or to put up with interference from anyone or anything at all. Perhaps this characteristic is one of the reasons why it is in the north, in the most inhospitable regions, that so many of Spain's famous monasteries stand, and why this area has produced many of Spain's mystics.

Sometimes the mountains slope steeply down into the sea, sometimes they open out into splendid wide valleys. It is an ideal area for camping in the summer. It is also on this coast that the history, or rather the pre-history, of Spain began; you can see the signs of it in the caves of Altamira, eleven miles from Santander on the road to Oviedo. It was the harbour that opened up this region; Santander's prosperity began after the discovery of America. It is still one of Spain's most florishing ports, and certainly its most beautiful one.

La Coruña has a beautiful boulevard along the sea with big white houses and glass conservatories; it is a crystal-line city at the very tip of the country, close to Cape Finisterre. You must go on further to Santiago de Compostela, named after St. James, who was buried here. He was the apostle who went out into the world to preach Christianity and so came to Spain. He is the Spanish saint *par excellence,* and the cry 'Santiago' (Saint James) was the battle cry of the Catholic Monarchs during the Reconquista. According to the legend, the grave of St. James was discovered by a man led by the star that led the Wise Men from the East to Bethlehem. James is supposed to have worked here for seven years and then to have returned to Israel, where he was beheaded. His body was then brought back to Galicia by his disciples. The star led later to the discovery of his grave, and that is how the town acquired the title 'Compostela' (in Latin, *campus stellae* the field of the star). The town is old and beautiful; it acquired a famous university and became the goal of pilgrimage. It has a fine cathedral in the Romanesque style. Extravagance and simplicity alternate here. When one sees the people in all their variety and liveliness rich men, merchants, customers, blind men and cripples one sees a good cross-section of the whole Spanish people.

On July 25 they celebrate the feast of St. James, and it is a sight worth seeing; then you will learn what a firework is really like!

On now to León, another old city, which takes its name from a Roman legion, the *Legio Septima Gemina.* There you must go inside the cathedral of Santa Maria de Regla, for it possesses what are probably the most beautiful stained-glass windows in the whole of Europe.

We finally leave Spain via Burgos. Burgos lies on a windy plateau in a hard climate; its cathedral is hard and sheer, too high above everything and inaccessible. The mortal remains of El Cid are buried in it. He has become a legend, the knight who loved his king and fought with him against the Moors, but through hurt pride turned away from him, went off to seek his own fortune with the help of the Moors and founded his own kingdom in Valencia. He remained loyal to his king and sent him gifts, but his pride demanded that the king should seek a reconciliation with him, not vice versa. And that came to pass, for the king married off the Cid's daughters to princes of the blood. Hise name is corruption of *Sidi,* the title by which the Moors addressed him. Now he lies with his wife, Doña Gimena, in the cathedral of Burgos.

Spain, a country full of contrasts, with a history in which the vicissitudes of fate and the will of man have trimphed in turn, where more blood has been spilt than anywhere else, and the men remain men because history has made clear to them what is only too human in man, is a land of which one therefore never tires. There, every facet of human existence both good and bad, gains another dimension, and that is why we end with the words of the poet Rafael Gonzales Castell:

> Die? Who speaks of dying!
> No, never die, Live!
> Fight, take your pleasure, work,
> And suffer and conquer,
> And now laugh,
> Now cry.

09511